Feel the Wind

Written and illustrated by Arthur Dorros

Thomas Y. Crowell   New York

for Sandra

Let's-Read-and-Find-Out Science Book is a registered
trademark of Harper & Row, Publishers, Inc.

Feel the Wind
Copyright © 1989 by Arthur Dorros
All rights reserved. No part of this book may be
used or reproduced in any manner whatsoever without
written permission except in the case of brief
quotations embodied in critical articles and reviews.
Printed in the United States of America.
For information address Thomas Y. Crowell Junior Books,
10 East 53rd Street, New York, N.Y. 10022.
Published simultaneously in Canada by
Fitzhenry & Whiteside Limited, Toronto.

1   2   3   4   5   6   7   8   9   10

First Edition

Library of Congress Cataloging-in-Publication Data
Dorros, Arthur.
  Feel the wind.

  (Let's-read-and-find-out science book)
  Summary: Explains what causes wind and how it affects
our environment. Includes instructions for making a
weathervane.
  1. Winds—Juvenile literature.   [1. Winds]   I. Title.
II. Series.
QC931.4.D67 1989   551.5'18   88-18961
ISBN 0-690-04739-8
ISBN 0-690-04741-X (lib. bdg.)

Feel the Wind

Have you felt the wind blowing through your hair? Wind is moving air. Air is what we breathe. It is everywhere around us, even though we can't see it.

We can't see air. And we can't really see the wind. But we can see the wind move things. Wind pushes clouds across the sky. Wind flutters the leaves of trees and makes ripples on lakes.

You can hear the wind too. When wind blows through
cracks in your house, it can sound like someone
whistling. If the wind blows very hard, it can sound like
a wild animal howling.

7

You can see the wind move things, you can hear the wind, and you can feel the wind too. Stand by an open window and let the breeze tickle your face.

A strong gust or a light breeze—wind is moving air. But what makes air move?

You can make air move with a fan, or by flapping a piece of cloth or paper. But fans don't make the wind.

What makes the wind that blows across fields and forests and mountains? What makes the wind that whips around tall buildings in the city?

All of the Earth is surrounded by air. Earth and the air around it are heated by the sun. But some parts of the Earth heat up more than other parts.

In the tropical parts of Earth, near the equator, the sun's rays strike the Earth directly. The air gets very hot.

Near the Earth's icy poles, the sun's rays strike at a slant. So the air stays cooler.

When hot air and cold air change places, wind is made.

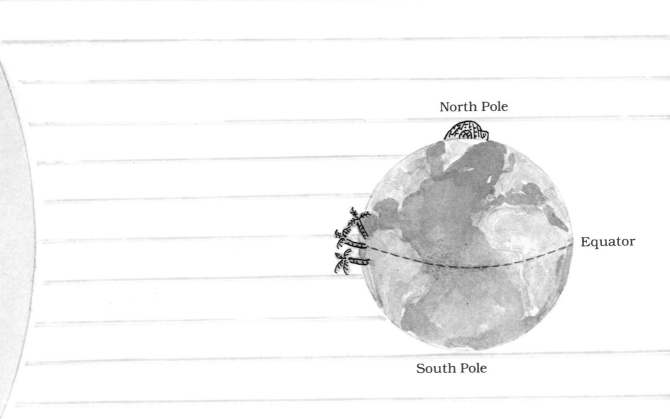

North Pole

Equator

South Pole

Hot air is lighter than cold air, so hot air rises.
People discovered this a long time ago and
used hot air to make balloons float.
The heated air in the balloons was
lighter than the cooler air outside.
The hot, light air made the balloons
float upward.

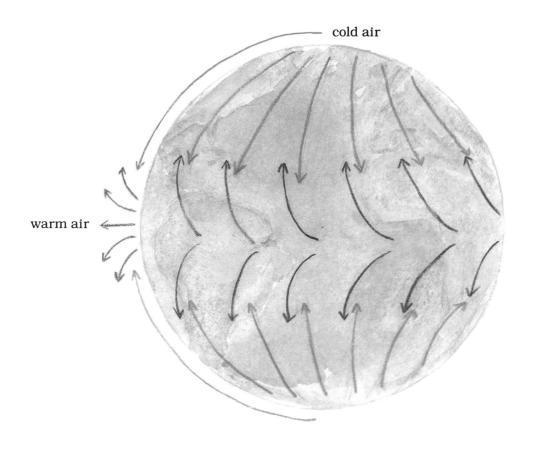

cold air

warm air

When heated air over the Earth rises, cooler, heavier air rushes in to take its place. The moving air is wind.

The sun's rays strike the equator directly. That's why it gets hotter there.

But some things get hotter than others because of what they are made of. You can discover this for yourself. Feel the sidewalk on a hot day. It is probably warmer than the grass beside it. The air above it is warmer, too. You might see shimmering heat waves as the hot air rises above the sidewalk.

Like the sidewalk and grass, land and water heat up differently too. On sunny summer days, the land gets warmer than the water. The air over the land also gets warmer.

The warm air rises, and cool winds blow in from the sea.

Some winds blow gently, others blow fast.
You can see how fast the winds are blowing by watching how things around you move. A gentle wind makes leaves dance.

A stronger wind might flap clothes on a line.

A very strong wind can make even heavy trees bend and sway.

Storms like hurricanes bring the strongest winds of all. Storm winds may blow very fast—more than 100 miles an hour. That's about twice as fast as cars go on the highway. These winds are strong enough to knock trees down.

You can see how strong the wind is by doing an experiment.

With a bicycle, stand so that the wind is blowing in your face.

Now ride into the wind. Feel how hard it is to pedal.

Then turn your bicycle around and ride with the wind pushing you along. Isn't it easier to pedal now?

The wind can carry your kite toward the clouds, or lift a glider.

Some birds can soar on the wind without moving their wings.

Sailboats are pushed along by the wind blowing against their sails.

People have used the power of moving air for thousands of years.

Windmills are wind-powered machines. The blades of a windmill turn when the wind pushes against them. The turning blades move other parts to lift water...

grind grain...

saw wood...

or make electricity.

Wind brings changes in the weather.
Rainstorms blow in with the wind...and out again
as the wind pushes the clouds along.

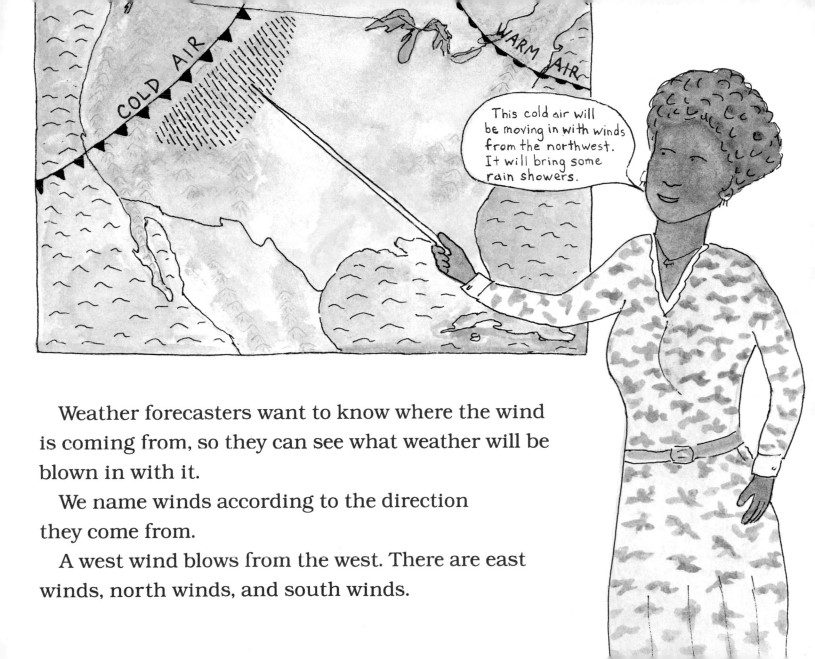

Weather forecasters want to know where the wind is coming from, so they can see what weather will be blown in with it.

We name winds according to the direction they come from.

A west wind blows from the west. There are east winds, north winds, and south winds.

In some parts of the world, people have given special names to the wind that blows there.

A chinook is a wind that blows from the Rocky Mountains of the United States. A chinook is so warm that in winter it can melt deep snow in just a few hours.

A sirocco is a hot, dry wind that blows from northern Africa.

You can figure out which way the wind is blowing by watching a leaf, a piece of cloth or string, or a weather vane.

The weather vane's arrow will point in the direction that the wind is coming from.

You can make your own weather vane like this...

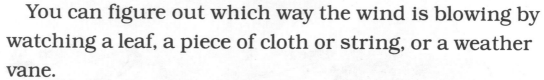

1. You will need:
   1 pencil
   (with eraser)
   1 pin
   1 straw
   1 piece of
      thick paper

   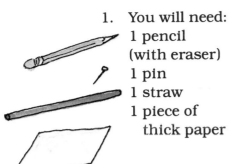

   And: scissors,
   a pen,
   and a stapler

   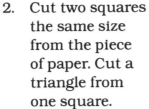

2. Cut two squares
   the same size
   from the piece
   of paper. Cut a
   triangle from
   one square.

   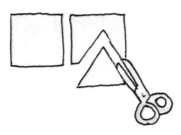

3. Staple the
   triangle on one
   end of the straw,
   and the square on
   the other end.

   staples

   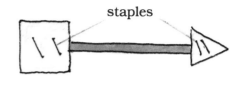

4. Balance the straw
   on your finger.

   Mark the
   balancing point
   with your pen.
   Then push the
   pin through the
   straw at the
   balancing point.

5. Push the pin into
   the eraser of the
   pencil. Push the
   pencil into the
   ground. Be careful
   to keep the pencil
   straight up
   and down.

6. Ask a grown-up
   for help placing
   markers around
   the pencil at
   north, south, east,
   and west.

When the wind blows, your weather vane will point in the direction the wind is blowing from.

Wind is moving air. All around us the wind is at work.
It carries the seeds of plants to new places where they
can take root and grow.

But powerful winds can also carry away the soil
plants need.

Wind can even change the strongest rocks. Bits of sand that the wind carries pound at the rocks and wear them away. The wearing away is called erosion. Some wind-eroded rocks have strange shapes.

Trees are shaped by the wind, and so are sand dunes.

The wind blows gently, the wind blows strong. See it, hear it, feel the wind.